THE WORLD OF
THE
HUNGER GAMES

by Kate Egan

Scholastic Press • Ne

ACKNOWLEDGMENTS

Many thanks to Yon Elvira, Amanda Maes, and Douglas Lloyd at Lionsgate; to David Levithan, Emily Seife, Erin Black, Lindsay Walter, and Rick DeMonico at Scholastic; and, as always, to the incomparable Suzanne Collins.

— K.E.

Published by Scholastic Press, an imprint of Scholastic Inc., *Publishers since 1920*.
SCHOLASTIC, SCHOLASTIC PRESS, and associated logos are trademarks and/or registered trademarks of Scholastic Inc.

Library of Congress Control Number: 2011945839

ISBN 978-0-545-42512-4

10 9 8 7 6 5 4 3 2 1   12 13 14 15 16 17/0

Printed in the U.S.A.   23
First edition, March 2012

This book was designed by Rick DeMonico and Heather Barber

TABLE OF CONTENTS

INTRODUCTION

You know this world, where it's easy to get confused between reality and reality TV.

You know this place, where rich and poor live side by side but worlds apart.

You, too, might question the choices a government makes on your behalf.

You, too, have seen the environment abused, damaged beyond repair.

This place is Panem, the world of *The Hunger Games*.

But it has roots in a world you know already: your own.

It's not that hard to imagine a path from here to there. That's part of what makes Suzanne Collins's trilogy so mesmerizing. Drawing on Roman history, Greek mythology, war stories, and her long experience as a scriptwriter and storyteller, Collins has created a dystopian world that feels at once foreign and unsettling yet familiar.

Now filmmakers have brought Collins's world to life in all its color and complexity.

If you're trying to get oriented — or if you already know the way — let this book be your guide to the world of *The Hunger Games*.

WELCOME
O PANEM

"In creating the Capitol I drew heavily on ancient Rome. You see the influence in everything from the Capitol citizens' names — Cinna, Claudius, Octavia — to the horse-drawn chariot procession through the streets, to the gladiator games."

— SUZANNE COLLINS

Long ago, this place was known as North America. That was before the droughts and the disasters, the storms and the fires, the floods and the war. That was before a powerful new force rose from the ashes to create order and rule with an iron hand.

Now this place is called Panem. It consists of twelve districts surrounding one shining Capitol.

The Capitol is Panem's seat of power and its largest city. Nestled in a mountain range once called the Rockies, it towers above the districts and is accessible only through long tunnels. The mountains protect the Capitol from intruders and insulate it from the districts.

The districts contain sparkling waters, lush forests, majestic mountains — and miserable people. These people fish those waters, fell those forests, and mine those mountains, all to meet the Capitol's needs. But there is no feast quite big enough, no fashion quite new enough for the Capitol. The people of the districts give their labor — they give their lives — all to feed the Capitol's insatiable appetites. Meanwhile, people are starving.

Some districts are favored by the Capitol: those that produce weapons and luxury goods. There, at least, the people have enough to eat. But even they have no opportunity beyond what the Capitol dictates.

Under such conditions, you might expect a revolution.

> "The name of the country, Panem, comes from the Latin phrase *panem et circenses*, which translates into 'bread and circuses.' In exchange for free bread and entertainment, the Roman population gave up both their political power and their responsibility."
>
> — SUZANNE COLLINS

That's been tried before. During the Dark Days, the districts attempted rebellion. All were defeated, and one — District 13 — was destroyed. Now it's a smoldering ruin, a reminder of what happens to those who defy the Capitol.

The annual Hunger Games are another reminder. Every year, each district sends two tributes, a boy and a girl, to compete in a fight to the death on live TV. The message is clear. In retribution for the long-ago rebellion, the Capitol will take whatever it wants from the people of the districts. Even the lives of their children.

The victor of the Hunger Games receives riches for life. His or her district is showered with gifts. Really, though, the Capitol is always the true winner.

Panem is a place of nightmares, but it's also a place we can understand, with its intractable injustices and its fine line between reality and "reality" as created for a broadcast. It's like the world as we know it — gone terribly wrong.

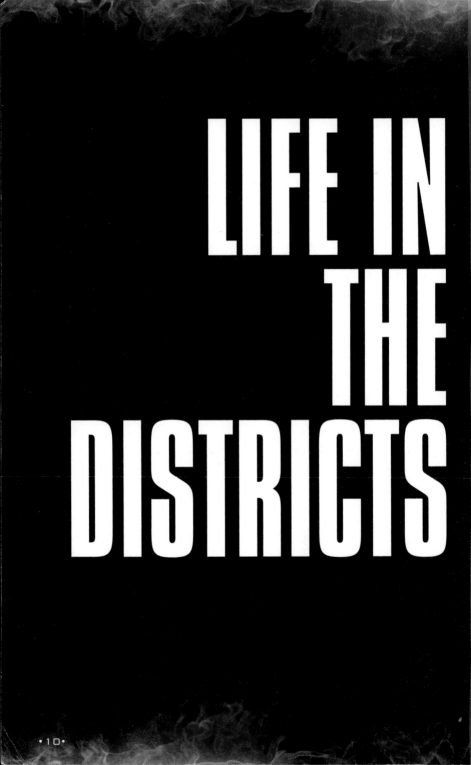

LIFE IN THE DISTRICTS

"But you have fruits and vegetables, right? Isn't [District] 11 all farms?"

"Oh, we never get that fancy stuff. That goes to the Capitol. I never tasted it 'til I got 'picked.'"

— KATNISS EVERDEEN AND RUE

The districts of Panem share borders and waterways, a language and a government, but they're completely isolated from one another. Fences surround each district. Cargo trains traverse the country carrying goods, but the distribution of goods is all controlled by the Capitol.

Most people never leave their home districts. The Capitol makes sure of that.

So though they share a language, communication between districts is difficult and dangerous. As a result, each district has developed distinct customs of its own. In District 12, for instance, it's a sign of respect to the dead to touch three fingers to your lips and then release them. In other districts, local customs are closely tied to whatever the assigned industry is.

Most of what the districts know about one another comes from the annual broadcast of the Hunger Games. Viewers see glimpses of other town squares during the reapings. They learn a little about the habits of the other districts as they watch the tributes in the arena.

The Hunger Games are what passes for shared history among the people of Panem. One district will know nothing about the living conditions or latest news in the adjoining district, but people in both will remember the year the arena was a frozen tundra, or the year seventeen tributes died on the first day.

That's because everybody — everywhere — is required to watch the Games.

Each district is dedicated to a particular industry, a particular task for the Capitol. Some districts make goods that are in great demand in the city. Other districts deliver raw materials or food.

While the districts produce things, the Capitol consumes them as fast as it can. Fads come and go quickly in the Capitol — it's the districts' job to create whatever the Capitol wants at any given moment. The people of the Capitol have never known hunger. They don't know about recycling, or care about sustainability. They want what's new and what's easy, whatever the cost to the districts.

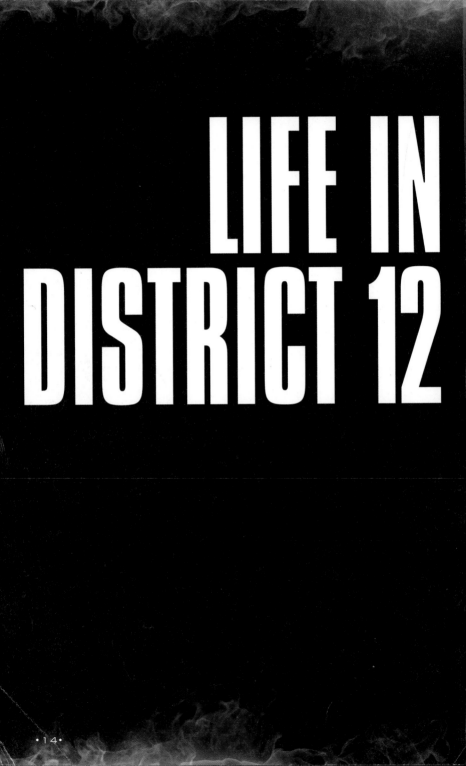

LIFE IN DISTRICT 12

"When I was younger, I scared my mother to death, the things I would blurt out about District 12, about the people who rule our country, Panem, from the far-off city called the Capitol. Eventually I understood this would only lead us to more trouble. So I learned to hold my tongue and to turn my features into an indifferent mask so that no one could ever read my thoughts."

— KATNISS EVERDEEN
THE HUNGER GAMES

District 12 is Panem's mining center, in a place that used to be called Appalachia. It is the poorest, least populated district — and the home of Katniss Everdeen, the female tribute in the Seventy-fourth annual Hunger Games.

In District 12, the miners leave before sunrise to descend deep into the earth. They return after nightfall, if they return at all. Mine explosions, like the one that killed Katniss's father, are common. At least once a year, though, the miners know they will see daylight. That's on the day of the reaping, when the tributes for the Hunger Games are chosen.

Most days, though, the miners return after dark to their houses in a scruffy neighborhood called the Seam, pushed to the edge of town. The district's few merchants live closer to the center of town, set apart from the very poor. Even within the district, there is tension between the haves and the have-nots.

In each district there's a Victor's Village, built to house the district's Hunger Games winners in luxury. These days, the population of District 12's Village is exactly one, and he's rarely seen in public.

Conditions in District 12 are dismal. Everything is falling apart, then patched back together. Since the district's so poor, the Capitol doesn't pay it much attention.

Electricity is scarce here, which makes life difficult for the locals. But it also means that the power that feeds the electric confinement fences around the district is rarely on. That allows a brave few to find a way to fend for themselves.

Here, the Capitol's police — the Peacekeepers — mingle quite freely with the people. They're not friends, exactly, but they're not enemies either.

There's an abandoned warehouse in town that once held coal, before the Capitol created a new system that transports the coal directly from the mines to the Capitol. There, the people of District 12 trade essentials in a black market they call the Hob. To an outsider, this place seems like a junk shop. To the people here, it's a lifeline. Markets like this are against the law, yet even the Peacekeepers come here for goods.

While the Capitol looks the other way, a person might just gain a measure of freedom.

PEOPLE OF DISTRICT 12

"Our part of District 12, nicknamed the Seam, is usually crawling with coal miners heading out to the morning shift at this hour. Men and women with hunched shoulders, swollen knuckles, many who have long since stopped trying to scrub the coal dust out of their broken nails, the lines of their sunken faces."

— KATNISS EVERDEEN
THE HUNGER GAMES

MINERS LEAVE THE SEAM TOGETHER EVERY MORNING.

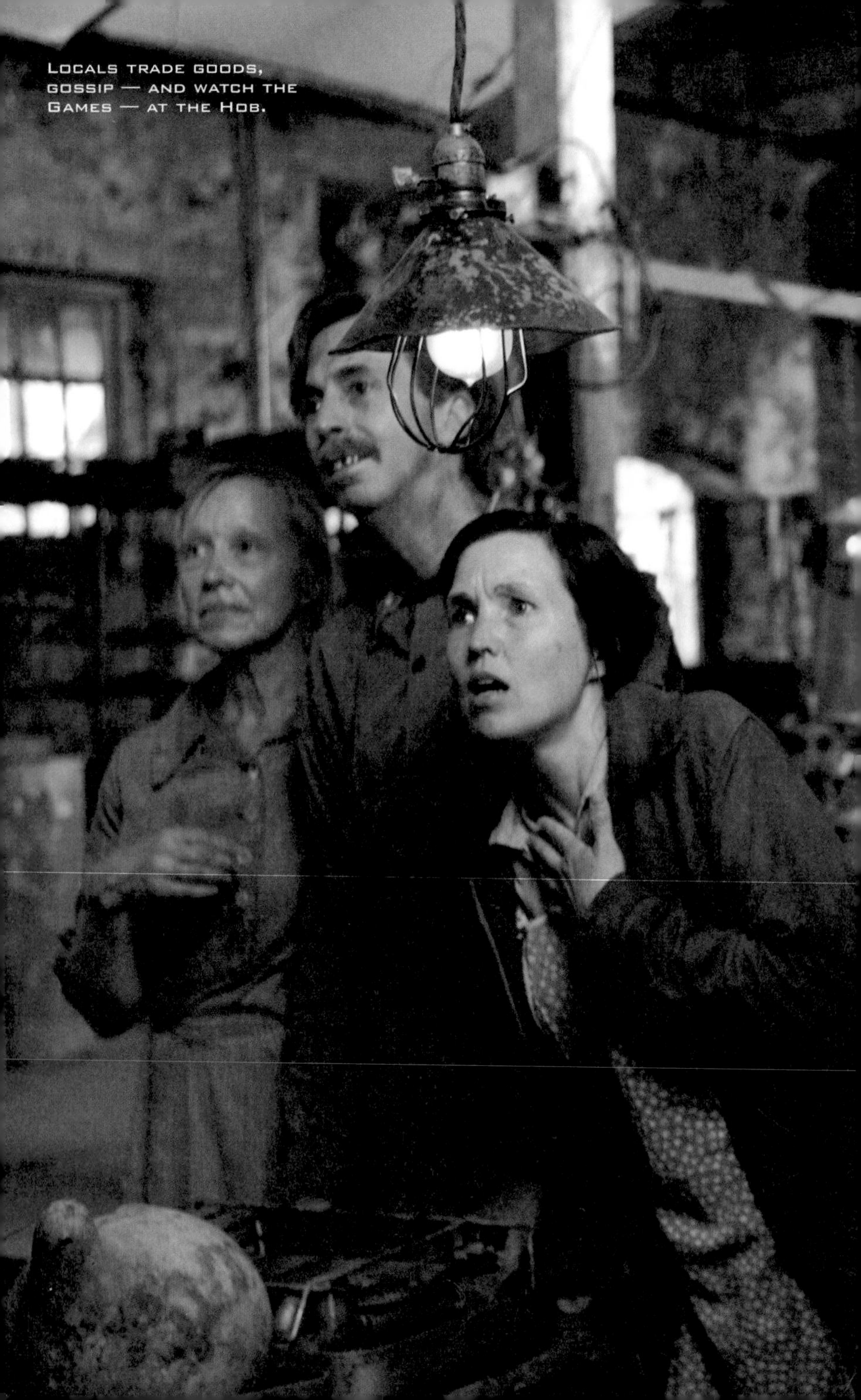

Locals trade goods, gossip — and watch the Games — at the Hob.

Gale Hawthorne is Katniss's best friend and hunting partner.

PEETA MELLARK'S FAMILY OWNS THE
BAKERY IN TOWN; HE ALWAYS HAS
PLENTY TO EAT.

RIES

HAYMITCH ABERNATHY IS DISTRICT 12'S ONLY LIVING HUNGER GAMES VICTOR.

HE IS A NOTORIOUS DRUNK.

It is his job to guide the district's tributes through the Games.

KATNISS
EVERDEEN

"We could do it, you know. Take off. Live in the woods. That's what we do anyway."

"They'd catch us."

"Maybe not."

— GALE HAWTHORNE AND KATNISS EVERDEEN

She may be only sixteen, but Katniss Everdeen is the head of her family.

She was eleven when her father died in the coal mines. The father who provided for his family. The father who taught her to hunt and to sing.

When he died, it was as if Katniss and her sister, Prim, lost both parents at once. Their mother's grief was so deep that she was unable to care for her daughters. She was unable to do anything except huddle in an old chair, staring into space, shut off from the world around her.

While she stared, her daughters almost starved.

Then, one rainy night, Katniss lingered longingly near the bakery, dizzy with hunger. Her classmate Peeta Mellark was baking bread inside. Then he was distracted for a moment, and the bread burned.

Katniss froze as his mother berated him, hit him, and ordered him to throw the bread to their pigs. But a small miracle happened: Peeta threw it to Katniss instead. And that night, Katniss and her family feasted on the hearty bread.

The next morning felt almost like spring. Katniss caught sight of a dandelion — an edible weed — growing from the dirt.

In that moment, Katniss knew what she'd do next. Her father had taught her what plants were safe to eat. He had

> "Look what I brought you. It's a mockingjay. To protect you. You wear that pin and nothing bad can happen to you. I promise."
> — KATNISS EVERDEEN

taught her how to hunt for game. She knew these activities were forbidden . . . yet it was her only chance for survival. And she was brave enough to take the risk.

Every day now, Katniss sneaks into forbidden territory beyond the fence. She hunts for game; she nets fish; she slips eggs out of nests; she gathers edible plants that are growing wild.

She keeps what she needs, then sells the rest at the Hob. Whatever it takes to keep her family going.

Katniss is an expert with a bow and arrows, such a neat shot that she never damages an animal's skin. Instead, she shoots it straight through the eye.

Things are better at home now. Katniss's mother is a healer, helping the sick and wounded. But Katniss can never forget the way things were. With her mother, she's always on edge.

It's not that way with Prim. Her little sister is the only person Katniss is sure — absolutely sure — that she loves.

"But what if they did? . . . What if everyone just stopped watching?"

"But they won't, Gale."

"But if they did. What if we did?"

"Won't happen."

"It's like a train wreck, Katniss. You may not want to watch, but you do. That's how they win. . . . If no one watches, then they don't have a game. It's as simple as that."

— GALE HAWTHORNE
AND KATNISS EVERDEEN

She loves her friend Gale, too, but in a different way. Not a romantic way, like you might expect. Gale is Katniss's hunting partner and best friend — with him, she can be herself. When they're together in the woods, they're almost free.

Gale dares to say what nobody else says about the cruelty and injustice of the Capitol. Sometimes he thinks that he and Katniss could survive if they ran away. Together.

Katniss listens, but she's not running anywhere. She's too practical for that. She doesn't think it would work, anyway. The Capitol's too strong.

But Katniss is also strong — stronger than she knows. And as she will discover, she's the ultimate survivor.

AT HOME WITH KATNISS EVERDEEN

"At eleven years old, with Prim just seven, I took over as head of the family. There was no choice."

— KATNISS EVERDEEN
THE HUNGER GAMES

THE EVERDEEN FAMILY LIVES
ON THE EDGE OF THE SEAM.

No miners live in this cottage now. There are only three remaining Everdeens: Katniss, her mother, and Katniss's sister, Primrose.

KATNISS UNEXPECTEDLY BECAME THE HEAD OF HER HOUSEHOLD. SHE HUNTS FOR GAME TO FEED HER FAMILY.

KATNISS'S FATHER HAS BEEN GONE FOR FIVE YEARS NOW, KILLED IN A MINE EXPLOSION.

Katniss's mother fell into a deep depression when her husband died.

Primrose Everdeen, Katniss's sister, is twelve. Katniss will do anything to protect her.

NOT FAR FROM KATNISS'S
HOUSE, THERE'S A WAY INTO
THE WOODS. THERE, NATURE'S
BEAUTY CAN ALMOST BLOCK
OUT THE MISERY ON THE
OTHER SIDE OF THE FENCE.

REAPING DAY

'War. Terrible war. Thirteen districts that rebelled against the country who fed them . . . loved them . . . protected them. When the traitors were defeated, we swore as a nation we would never know this treason again. And so it was decreed that each year the various districts shall offer up in tribute one brave young man and woman to fight to the death in a pageant of honor, courage, and sacrifice."

— CAPITOL FILM

On the day of the reaping, the people of each district gather in their town square. In District 12, the square is really just an old rail yard, with a warehouse attached, but once a year it's transformed by TV lights, video screens, and an anxious crowd. The miners emerge, blinking, into the open space.

It's a day that everybody dreads, and the reality is even worse than the anticipation.

The decorations are festive, but the looks on people's faces give the truth away: Two children are about to be sent away to die. Is it worse to be the person sent or the family left behind?

Silently, the gathered people watch a movie on the video screens. It's about the failed rebellion and the rise of Panem. The same movie every year. Deadly dull and endless propaganda.

Then a representative from the Capitol draws names from two glass balls. In District 12, this person is Effie Trinket. In the drab world of this district, her bright hair, her outrageous clothes, and her Capitol accent really stand out. She chooses one boy and one girl, both between the ages of twelve and eighteen, to be the district's tributes in the Games.

Not every child has the same chance of being chosen in the drawing. Poorer children purchase tesserae, meaning

> "It's your first year, Prim. Your name's only in there once. They're not gonna pick you."
>
> — KATNISS EVERDEEN

that their names are entered an extra time in exchange for a supply of food. Some, like Katniss and Gale, have multiple tesserae. Many of the paper slips in the ball have their names on them.

In the Capitol, the reaping kicks off weeks of good times. Each district's reaping is broadcast live, and eager viewers get their first look at the Games' contestants.

In the richer districts, it's an honor to compete in the Hunger Games. Some boys and girls have been training their whole lives to go into the arena, and if they are not chosen in the reaping, they volunteer to replace whoever was. These kids — from Districts 1 and 2 — are known in the poorer districts as the Career Tributes.

In most districts, though — and certainly in District 12 — the reaping is a somber occasion. A final good-bye.

THE PEOPLE OF DISTRICT 12 GATHER IN THE SQUARE FOR THE REAPING.

"HAPPY HUNGER GAMES!" cheers Effie Trinket. "AND MAY THE ODDS BE EVER IN YOUR FAVOR!"

SHE APPROACHES THE REAPING BALLS AND DRAWS THE NAMES.

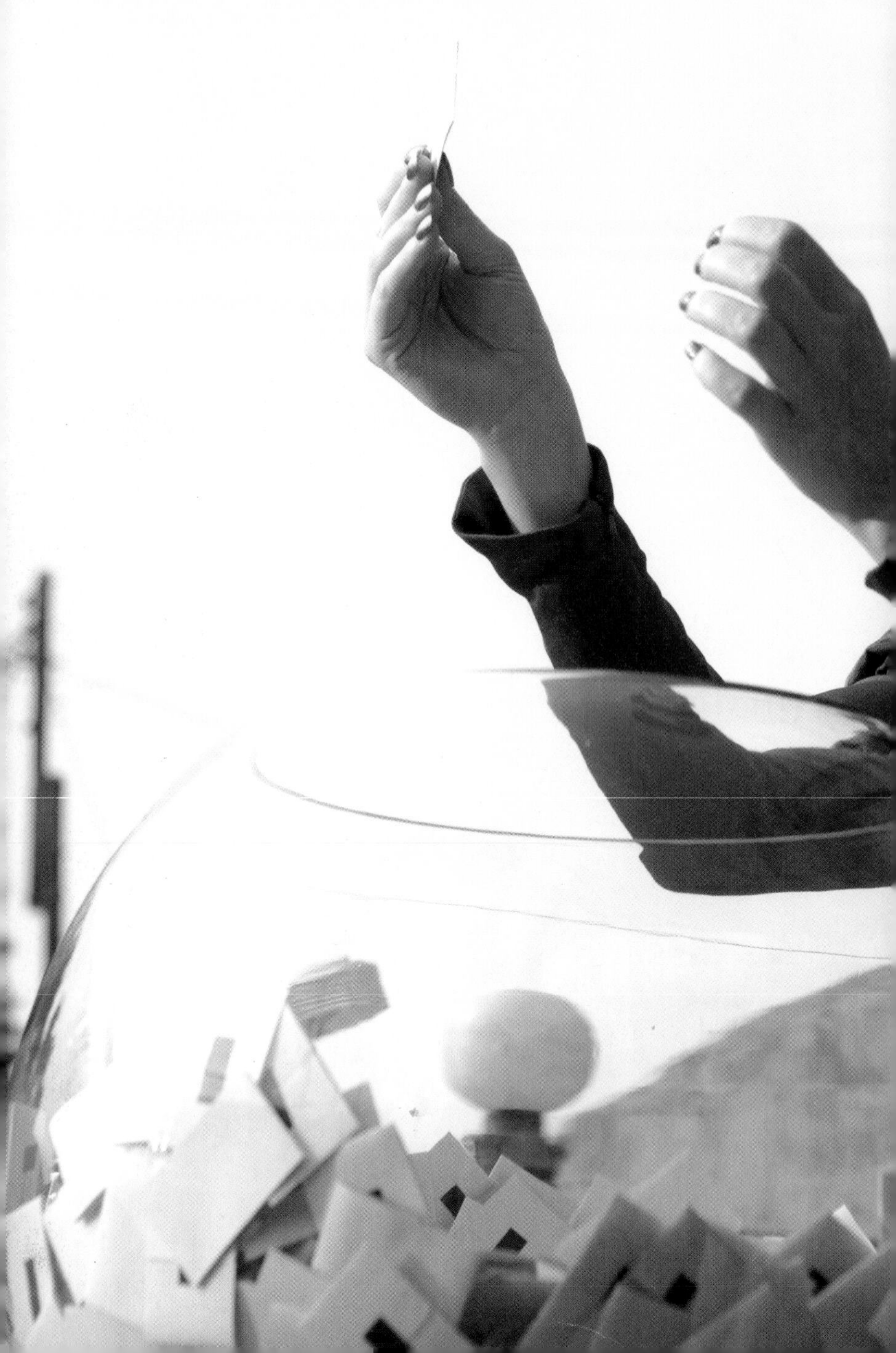

THIS YEAR, THE GIRL'S NAME IS PRIMROSE EVERDEEN.

INSTINCTIVELY, KATNISS SPRINGS FORWARD TO TAKE HER SISTER'S PLACE. "I VOLUNTEER!" SHE CALLS OUT.

PRIM WON'T LET HER
SISTER GO . . .

. . . UNTIL GALE COMES TO CARRY HER AWAY.

Gale promises to take care of Katniss's family. She would do the same for him.

Then, with Peeta, the male tribute, Katniss boards the train to the Capitol. It's her first glimpse of a lavish world she's never seen before, with more food than she could ever eat.

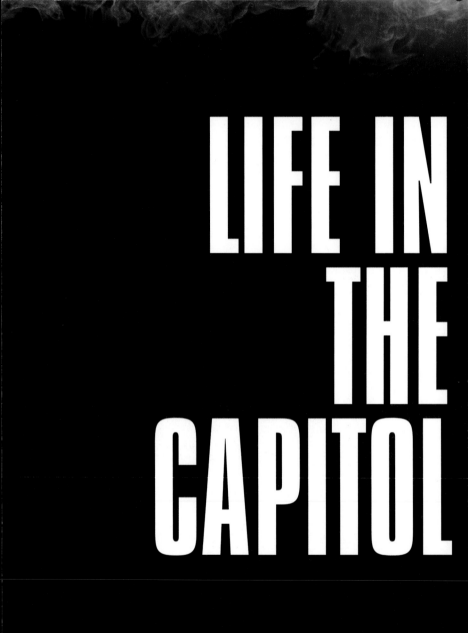

LIFE IN THE CAPITOL

"Since she was eleven years old, Katniss has spent every day preoccupied with how to feed her family. Starvation is a constant threat in the districts. The Capitol uses food, or lack thereof, as a weapon. One of the goals of the Hunger Games is to remind the oppressed districts that a full stomach is synonymous with power. The extravagance of the food the tributes encounter in the Capitol only drives this home."

— SUZANNE COLLINS

In the Capitol, appearances are everything. You can see it in the powerful architecture of the buildings and in the design of the city, which showcases the Capitol's might. You can see it in the local fashion, too.

To an outsider, the people of the Capitol look outlandish. Bizarre. Here, color is the name of the game. It works for hair, of course, but also for lips — for skin — for pets. Here, people know there's nothing in nature that can't be improved by plastic surgery or a decorative tattoo.

"What do they do all day, these people in the Capitol, besides decorating their bodies and waiting around for a new shipment of tributes to roll in and die for their entertainment?"

— KATNISS EVERDEEN
THE HUNGER GAMES

People move slowly through the streets of the Capitol — they have no jobs, no place important to go. But when the Hunger Games are on, it's a different story.

Then there's a whirl of parties, a sense of drama. Everyone has a favorite tribute and money riding on the outcome. Who will live and who will die? How will they kill their opponents? People can even participate in the Games directly by becoming sponsors and sending life-saving supplies into the arena.

Viewers are caught up in the story and the contest, ignoring the young lives tragically lost. For most people in the Capitol, the Games are just . . . games.

The people of the Capitol are not all cruel. They are ignorant and shallow, and most know little of what life is like in the districts. They don't even think to ask.

IN THE CAPITOL, THE
FEASTS ARE DECADENT
AND THE HOMES ARE
LUXURIOUS.

IT'S IMPORTANT TO LOOK YOUR BEST IN THE CAPITOL. THAT MEANS BRIGHT AND SHINY, LIKE PLASTIC.

No head looks right without a hat! The bigger, the better.

THE STYLISTS AND
CAPITOL RESIDENTS
LINE THE STREETS
TO SEE THE PARADE
OF THE TRIBUTES.

Viewers pay close attention to all the tributes as they go by.

"That's an amazing thing to see. Even though they're 'opponents,' here they are, sharing this triumphal moment together."
— Claudius Templesmith

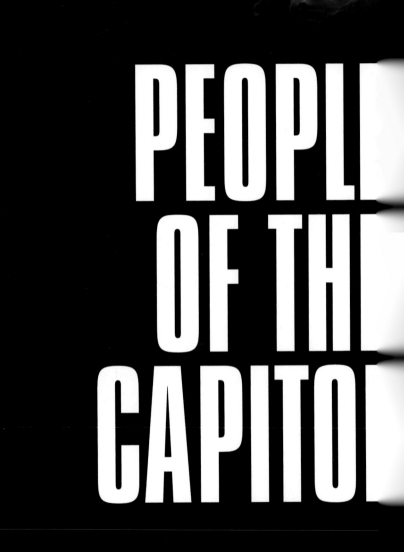

PEOPLE
OF THE
CAPITOL

"If there's not an audience, there's not a gladiator game. It's a necessary component. The event is a form of popular entertainment. The audiences for both the Roman games and today's reality TV shows are almost characters in themselves. They can respond with great enthusiasm or they can play a role in your elimination."

— SUZANNE COLLINS

FLAVIUS AND VENIA MAKE KATNISS
BEAUTIFUL — IN THEIR OWN WAY.

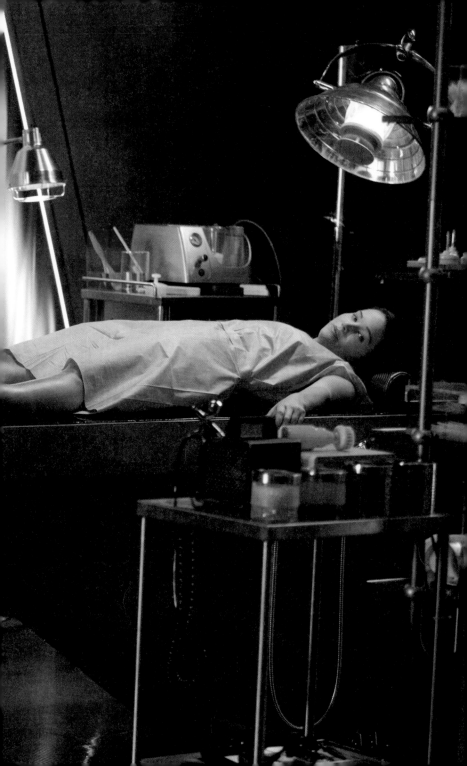

CINNA UNDERSTANDS
WHAT REALLY MAKES
KATNISS BEAUTIFUL.

FROM HIS BALCONY,
PRESIDENT SNOW
OBSERVES THIS
YEAR'S TRIBUTES.

IN THE GAMES CENTER
CONTROL ROOM, SENECA
CRANE AND THE GAMEMAKERS
PUT THE FINAL TOUCHES ON
THEIR PLANS.

CAESAR FLICKERMAN
INTERVIEWS THE TRIBUTES
ONE BY ONE . . .

. . . AND BANTERS FOR THE
CAMERAS. HE'S SO GOOD AT
MAKING THE TRIBUTES FEEL
AT EASE.

Some tributes don't feel as comfortable in the limelight, though.

TRIBUTES IN THE CAPITOL

"Seneca, why do you think we have a winner? If we just wanted to intimidate the districts, why not round up twenty-four of them at random and execute them all at once? . . . Hope. It's the only thing stronger than fear. But it's also delicate. It can get out of control. Like a fire. A little hope is effective. A lot of hope is dangerous. The spark is fine as long as it's contained."

— PRESIDENT SNOW

When Katniss arrives in the Capitol, she is blinded by the colors and the luxury, overwhelmed by the buffets at every meal. Just as bewildering as what she sees, though, is what she feels. Suddenly, she's thrust into a world where there's nobody she can trust.

Venia and Flavius hose her down and begin to transform her into a person that Capitol viewers will want to watch. Katniss isn't sure what's more scary: the way they look or the way they want her to look. Cutting, scrubbing, tweezing, polishing, and painting are all part of the process.

Cinna, her stylist, treats her kindly. He apologizes for what he has to do. He creates a look that makes Katniss famous across Panem. Thanks to him, she will always be the Girl on Fire. But can an image maker be an ally? Or a friend?

President Coriolanus Snow welcomes the tributes to the Capitol from the balcony of his mansion. Katniss doesn't meet him right away, but she knows what he looks like. His kindly appearance masks a brutal strength that's allowed him to hold on to power for more than a quarter of a century. Anyone would notice the hard glint in his eye.

Every year, the Gamemakers design and manipulate a new arena and everything in it: the climate, the terrain, the traps. Whatever it takes to keep the audience on the edge of its seat. Seneca Crane is this year's Head Gamemaker,

> "We must seem like monsters to you. And . . . I'm sorry this happened to you. I'm here to help you in any way I can."
>
> — CINNA

and in many ways Katniss is the tribute of his dreams. An underdog, he realizes, is good for ratings.

Near the end of training, the Gamemakers observe the tributes individually, and score them according to their skills. Tributes with high scores will attract more sponsors.

Katniss knows that she has skills that could impress the Gamemakers. Yet they don't even have the decency to give her their attention. They hardly acknowledge her at all — until she takes matters into her own hands.

Each tribute is also interviewed by legendary Capitol personality Caesar Flickerman. He has been interviewing tributes for forty years! He's known for getting kids to open up to the audience. Charming tributes, again, will get more sponsors.

Caesar Flickerman and Claudius Templesmith are the announcers of the Games, the voices that the tributes and the audience will hear once the action begins.

Caesar fawns over Katniss during her interview. But his attention, like all the attention she's received in the Capitol, is loaded with ulterior motives. Like everything here, he's all about the show.

KATNISS'S APARTMENT IS FIT
FOR A QUEEN.

AVOXES TEND TO HER EVERY NEED.

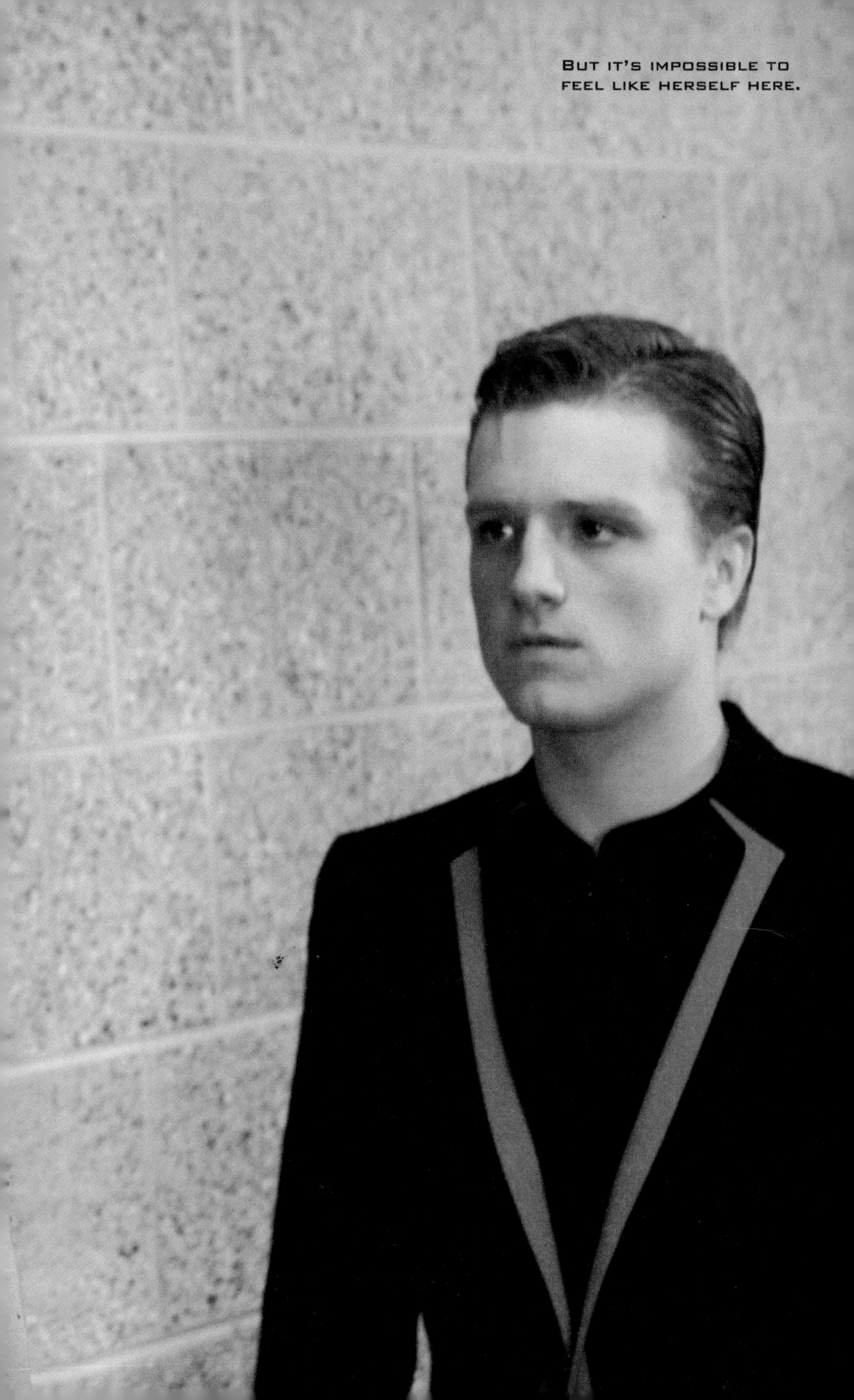
But it's impossible to
feel like herself here.

TRAINING FOR THE HUNGER GAMES

"You want to know how to really stay alive? You get people to like you. Oh. Not what you were expecting? Well, when you're in the middle of the Game — starving or freezing — some water, a knife, or even some matches could mean the difference between life and death. And those things only come from sponsors. And to get sponsors, you have to make people like you. And right now, sweetheart, you're not off to a real good start."

— HAYMITCH ABERNATHY

The tributes are given several days of training, right in the center in the Capitol, before the Hunger Games begin. They live in plush apartments decorated as if for royalty, with high ceilings and shining furniture. Using a remote control, Katniss can change the view she sees out the window.

Every meal is an over-the-top, all-you-can-eat buffet. Katniss has never seen so much food in her life. It would be even more enjoyable if she didn't know she was being fattened up for the slaughter.

The Training Center is a vast gym, with stations set up for learning different skills that the tributes might find useful in the arena. Building fires, finding shelter. Throwing knives and swinging swords. Camouflage and combat. Some are required, while others are optional — tributes can chose according to their interests and abilities.

There's an obstacle course, to test the tributes' strength and reflexes. And there are targets for practicing with knives and spears. These have human faces . . . just like the targets they'll face in the arena. Every once in a while, there's that stark reminder of what they're here for. Training isn't about getting stronger for its own sake. It's about preparing to kill, and preparing to die, on a national broadcast.

Some of the tributes are intimidating, while others seem almost nice. But Katniss is always aware that in the arena nobody will really be a friend.

The Training Center echoes with the sound of clanging weapons. But it also fills with a strange sort of hope, for, with every new skill gained, each tribute starts to believe — against all logic — that he or she might be the lucky one to come out of the arena alive.

It's an entirely false hope implanted by the Capitol to ensure that the Games are especially entertaining.

THE TRAINING CENTER IS A CAVERNOUS SPACE,
FILLED WITH EVERY WEAPON YOU CAN IMAGINE.

FROM A BALCONY ABOVE THE GYM, SENECA
CRANE AND THE GAMEMAKERS OBSERVE
THE TRIBUTES CAREFULLY.

ATALA, THE HEAD TRAINER, EXPLAINS SOME RULES TO THE TRIBUTES.

THEY HURTLE THROUGH AN
OBSTACLE COURSE.

THRESH IS BRIMMING WITH BRUTE STRENGTH.

THE FEMALE TRIBUTE FROM DISTRICT 3 GETS HURT DURING TRAINING.

RUE IS QUIET AND STEALTHY.

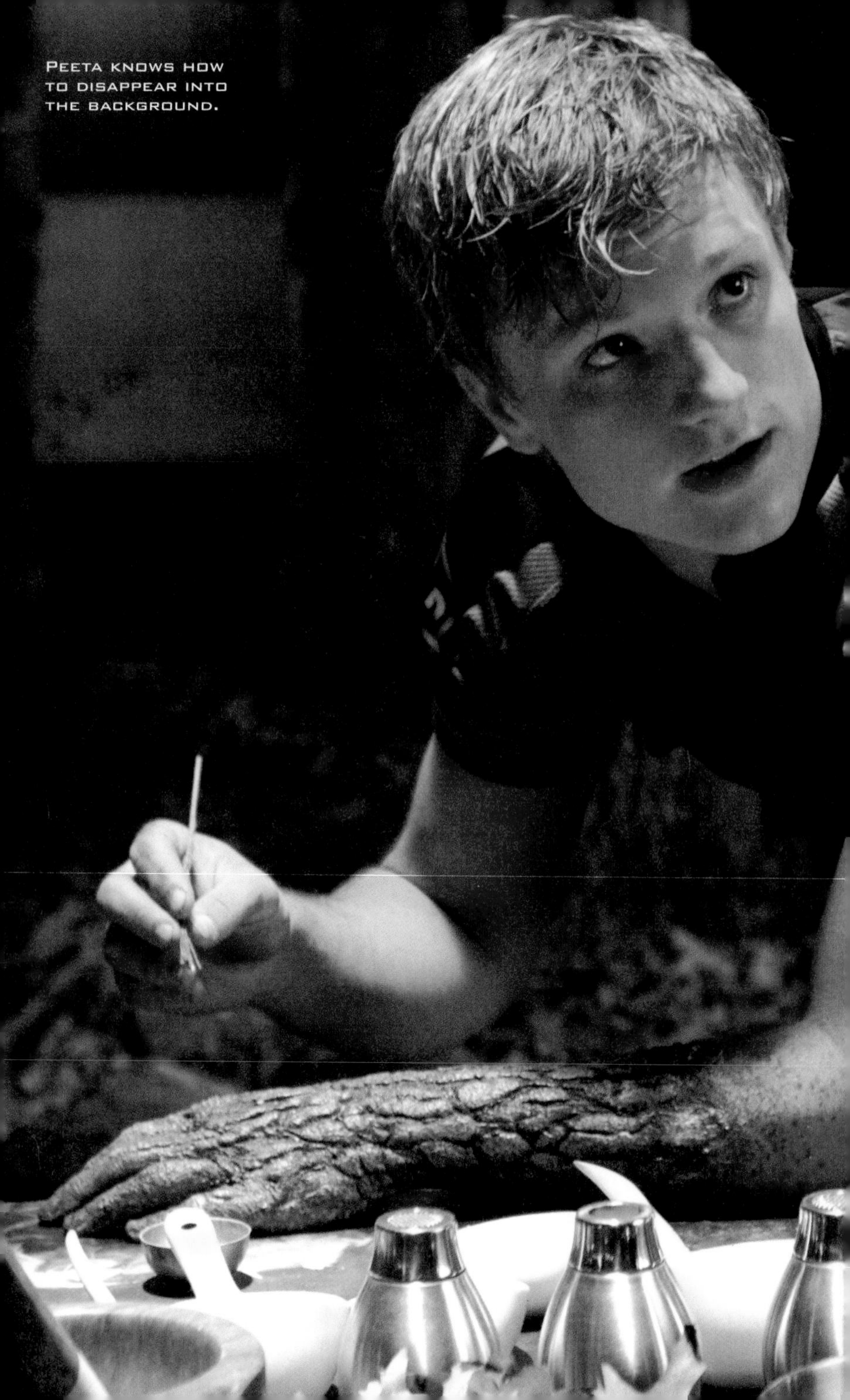

PEETA KNOWS HOW TO DISAPPEAR INTO THE BACKGROUND.

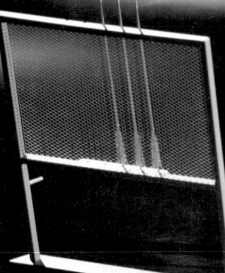

EACH TRIBUTE GETS A PRIVATE AUDIENCE
WITH THE GAMEMAKERS.

THEY SEEM MORE INTERESTED IN THEIR FOOD THAN IN KATNISS . . . UNTIL SHE TRIES SOMETHING EXTRAORDINARY.

WHEN TRAINING IS OVER,
A HOVERCRAFT CARRIES
THE TRIBUTES AWAY FROM
THE CAPITOL.

THEY STAND POISED IN A SEMICIRCLE, WAITING FOR THE FINAL COUNTDOWN TO END.

LET THE SEVENTY-FOURTH
HUNGER GAMES BEGIN!

CREATURES
OF PANEM

"... I realize what else unsettled me about the mutts. The green eyes glowering at me are unlike any dog or wolf, any canine I've ever seen. They are unmistakably human."

— KATNISS EVERDEEN
THE HUNGER GAMES

In past years, the Capitol has unleashed some of its most terrifying muttations, or genetically altered animals, at the Hunger Games. The arena is the best place to showcase what science and technology can do to keep Panem's people in their proper place. Muttations are intended to be intimidating and often lethal.

Tracker jackers are genetically altered wasps, programmed to kill anyone who disturbs their nest. They're bigger than regular wasps, and their stings raise huge welts on the skin, roughly the size of plums. Tracker jacker venom creates hallucinations, even madness.

Wolf mutts are part human, part wolf. What makes them terrifying is that their human DNA comes from tributes in the Hunger Games. They can walk on their hind legs and jump extremely high, slashing with their four-inch claws. They are deadly, furious beasts.

Once in a while, though, nature interferes with the Capitol's plans.

During the rebellion, the Capitol developed jabberjays — birds that could memorize and repeat human conversations — to use as spies. The rebels turned the birds against the Capitol by deliberately telling them lies.

Soon jabberjays were no longer useful to the Capitol, but those remaining created a new species when they mated with mockingbirds. Mockingjays can pick up songs

"The muttations or 'mutts' fall into two categories. The first includes creatures that have been genetically designed to perform as some type of weapon, like the tracker jackers in *The Hunger Games*. The second are what I think of as alpha mutts. They, as Katniss mentions in *Mockingjay*, incorporate a perverse psychological twist designed to terrify the victim. Each book in the series contains one alpha mutt. Each of these mutts relies on a particular sense — sight, hearing, or smell — to unhinge the individual it's targeted to destroy."

— SUZANNE COLLINS

very quickly and relay them back. In District 11 they're used to pass signals along through the orchards. The mockingjays are not mutts, exactly, and they're not dangerous. They're just . . . surprising.

PERILS OF THE HUNGER GAMES

"Each of you needs
something desperately
and this is home cooking,
my friends. If you decide
to come — you will find
exactly what you need.
To save yourself or . . .
someone you care about."

— CLAUDIUS TEMPLESMITH

Inside the arena, the tributes will face many challenges. Some are designed by the Gamemakers to separate the strong tributes from the weak. Some are designed to exploit tributes' characteristics and flaws. And all are designed to make sure the Capitol audience has an enthralling show to watch.

The Gamemakers aim to entertain the audience and create a spectacle that sponsors will want to be involved in. "Natural" disasters and terrifying mutts are par for the course.

Seneca Crane has his eye on Katniss, an entirely new kind of tribute. She comes from a poor district, so she hasn't been trained. The Careers have been training all their lives in special schools for this moment, and Katniss shouldn't stand a chance against them.

Yet she has that spark. She has that natural ability, sharpened by her time in the woods. The audience is drawn to her. Panem is rooting for an underdog!

At Seneca's direction, many of the obstacles are used to engage and showcase Katniss for the viewers back home. Suddenly, she's a star, and Seneca wants to make the most of her celebrity.

Only President Snow is thinking about what message it sends to the districts if, for once, the underdog actually wins.

He is keenly aware of the purpose of the Games: to keep the districts in line. An underdog is fine, in her place. But an underdog rising to the top is a different story altogether. A dangerous model for the districts. Somebody who must be destroyed . . . before it's too late.

THE CORNUCOPIA

At the Cornucopia, piles of essential weapons and supplies lie waiting for whichever tribute is brave — or foolish — enough to reach for them.

THE CORNUCOPIA

Fighting at the Cornucopia is always brutal.

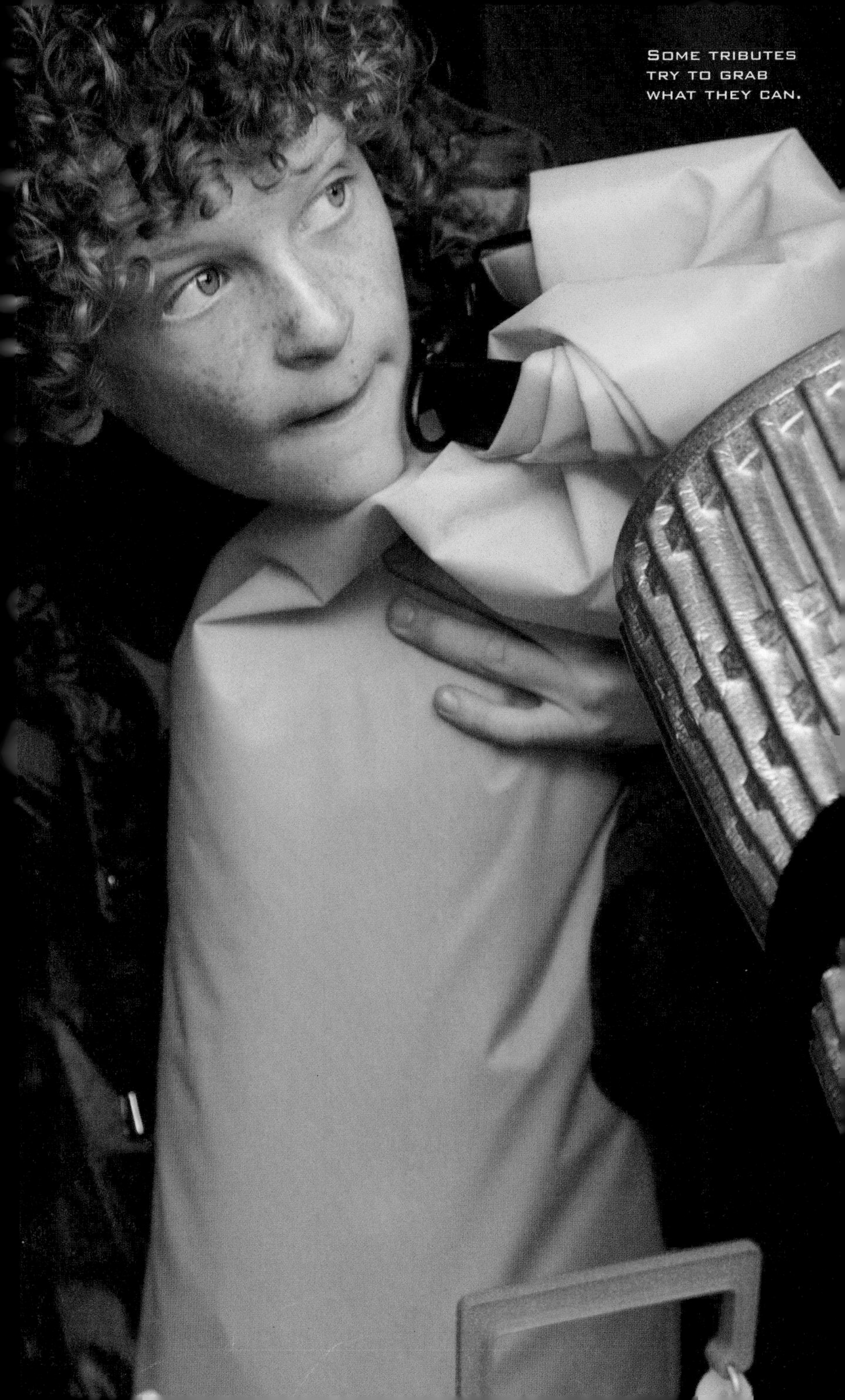
SOME TRIBUTES
TRY TO GRAB
WHAT THEY CAN.

FEAR

A PACK OF THE STRONGEST TRIBUTES IS PROWLING
TOGETHER, WORKING TO TAKE OUT ANYONE WHO'S
WEAK OR SEEMS TO BE A THREAT.

ONE OF THE PACK IS SOMEONE KATNISS
THOUGHT SHE COULD TRUST.

FEAR

Soon there's the sound of cannons, and images in the sky. Each blast marks a tribute's death. Katniss could be next. Tomorrow could be the day that she dies.

INJURIES

HOBBLED BY
BURNS FROM
FIREBALLS,
KATNISS
RESTS.

There are dangers all around. Sometimes they blend into the woods . . . until someone points them out.

INJURIES

There's a nest of tracker jackers just above her head. Katniss saws off the branch they're on, sending it down onto other tributes below. They all suffer the toxic sting.

"Those things are VERY lethal."

"For those of you who don't remember, it's genetically engineered venom that produces searing pain, and in extreme cases, death."

— CLAUDIUS TEMPLESMITH AND CAESAR FLICKERMAN

ALLIANCES

The Careers are still together, hoarding their supplies.

ALLIANCES

A tribute from District 3 is their ally . . . as long as his skills keep their supplies secure.

ALLIANCES

KATNISS AND RUE WORK TOGETHER . . .

. . . AND LEAVE THE CAREERS AT A LOSS.

ALLIANCES

"Deep in the meadow, under the willow
A bed of grass, a soft green pillow
Lay down your head, and close your sleepy eyes
And when again they open, the sun will rise.
Here it's safe, here it's warm
Here the daisies guard you from every harm
Here your dreams are sweet and tomorrow brings them true
Here is the place where I love you."

— District 12 Lullaby

DEFIANCE

SOMETHING IN KATNISS SNAPS. SHE
IS MORE THAN JUST A PIECE IN THESE
GAMES. ALL OVER PANEM, PEOPLE
WILL SEE HER PRIVATE REBELLION.

RULE CHANGES

THE VOICE OF CLAUDIUS
TEMPLESMITH RINGS OUT
ACROSS THE ARENA.
THERE'S BEEN A CHANGE
IN THE RULES. KATNISS
YELLS, "PEETA!"

SHE FINDS HIM CLEVERLY
DISGUISED, BUT NEAR
DEATH.

LOVE

To stay alive, Katniss and
Peeta stick together.

IN A CAVE, THEY CREATE WHAT
FEELS ALMOST LIKE A HOME.

LOVE

When she kisses Peeta, Haymitch sends things they need in silver parachutes.

LOVE

WITHIN THE GAMES, KATNISS
PLAYS A GAME OF HER OWN.

LIES

Claudius Templesmith promises each tribute whatever they need most desperately.

LIES

Katniss lies to Peeta to get
there, but she's been lied to
herself. To get what she came
for, she will have to fight.

LIES

AN UNINTENTIONAL DECEPTION
LEADS TO FOXFACE'S DEATH.

LAST MOVE

Katniss and Peeta have managed to evade death until now.

LAST MOVE

ONE FINAL RULE CHANGE
SNATCHES VICTORY AWAY
FROM THE PAIR.

"One of us has to die. They have to have their victor."

"No. No, they don't. Why should they?"

— PEETA MELLARK AND KATNISS EVERDEEN

LAST MOVE

THAT'S WHEN THEY CHANGE THE
RULES THEMSELVES. FOREVER.

"Now listen to me. When they ask you, you say you couldn't help yourself. You were so in love with this boy, the thought of being without him was unthinkable. You'd rather die than not be with him. Do you understand?"

— Haymitch Abernathy

Katniss's difficult life has made her practical and hard. Other girls her age might wonder about love, but Katniss isn't one of them. She doesn't have time for that. She's too busy looking for her family's next meal.

You wouldn't say she was cold, when she has such fierce love for her sister, such deep trust in her friend Gale. Gale is her best friend, her equal partner. With him, Katniss has a comfort and a trust she shares with nobody else. She never even thinks of wanting more. But she's wary of people, generally, and she's closed off to the possibility of romance in her life. Until — of all things — the Hunger Games begin to open her heart to new possibilities. When suddenly she has to say good-bye to Gale, she wonders for a moment . . . what could have been?

The Hunger Games are confusing on many levels. Katniss is constantly observed, judged, and exploited. She has to negotiate the Capitol's temptations and the arena's deprivations. Her emotions are on public display.

When Peeta tells the whole world he's always had a crush on her, Katniss assumes it's just a part of the Games. She is humiliated and angry until Haymitch explains that Peeta has made her look desirable. Katniss can appreciate the practical advantage of that. If Peeta likes her, maybe sponsors will, too.

Midway through the Games, a change in the rules

pushes these tributes closer together. Katniss is willing to play by this new decree. As always, she will do what she needs to survive. It doesn't take her long to realize she will get help from Haymitch if she acts like she and Peeta are in love.

As she cares for Peeta, nursing him back to health, she begins to care in a different way, too. Sometimes she is acting. Sometimes she wonders if Peeta is acting, too. But sometimes they are caught up in something unmistakably honest and real.

In the midst of sheer horror, unfamiliar feelings flicker inside Katniss. But just as the Capitol robs children of their lives, it will also rob her of the sweetness of first love. Her feelings aren't simple, and they're not entirely her own. Instead, they're wrapped up with her own survival and — always — how they will appear to an audience.

AFTER THE GAMES

"What happens when we get back?"

"I don't know. I guess we try to forget."

"I don't want to forget."

— PEETA MELLARK AND KATNISS EVERDEEN

Back in the Capitol, the show goes on. Though they've left the arena, Katniss and Peeta are still constantly in the camera's gaze. They are again interviewed by Caesar Flickerman — another performance. Their outfits, their makeup, their loving words — how much is real, and how much is for the audience?

Katniss is reunited with Haymitch. Her mentor. Her partner in crime.

And now Katniss realizes that's what it is. She's always known it's a crime that there are Games at all, of course. But it's also an unforgivable crime that she has embarrassed the Capitol in such a public way, and at its proudest moment.

When President Snow crowns her as victor, she can see the twist of his false and angry smile.

Katniss will be going home on the train, back to her old life. She'll see her family — and Gale. But will anything be the same?

This is not an ending. It's only a beginning. Like a mockingjay, Katniss has survived against the odds, and like a mockingjay, she's an anomaly. Now the Capitol will be closely watching the heroine it has unintentionally created.

"They aren't happy with you."

"Why? 'Cause I didn't die?"

"Because you showed them up."

"Well, I'm sorry it didn't go the way they planned. You know I'm not very happy with them, either."

"This is serious, Katniss. And not just for you."

". . . My family?"

"They don't take these things lightly."
— HAYMITCH ABERNATHY
AND KATNISS EVERDEEN

PRESIDENT SNOW CROWNS
THE TWO VICTORS.

IN AN INTERVIEW WITH CAESAR
FLICKERMAN, KATNISS AND
PEETA PROCLAIM THEIR TRUE
LOVE TO ALL OF PANEM.

THE HUNGER GAMES GLOSSARY

Abernathy, Haymitch: Only living victor from District 12, so is assigned to mentor District 12 tributes in the Hunger Games every year.

Atala: Head trainer in the Capitol's Training Center. Teaches skills that tributes might find useful in the arena.

Avoxes: People who have committed crimes and had their tongues cut out as punishment. Work as servants in the Capitol.

Buttercup: Prim's mangy yellow cat. Loved by Prim, but not by Katniss.

Capitol, the: Main city and seat of power in the country of Panem.

Capitol residents: Favor brightly dyed hair and eccentric clothing. Speak in a distinctive accent, with a hissing "s" and ends of sentences rising, as if in question. Enthusiastic spectators of the Hunger Games.

Career Tributes (aka the Careers): Teens who have trained their whole lives, and attended special schools, in order to compete in the Hunger Games. Those not chosen in reapings volunteer to take the place of those who are.

Cato: Boy tribute from District 2. Career. Huge, ruthless, and wily. Kills Thresh. Is one of the last tributes left standing. Almost devoured by mutts, until put out of his misery by Katniss.

Cinna: Katniss's stylist in the Capitol, responsible for creating her signature look and identity as the Girl on Fire. Does not look or dress like other Capitol residents. Is quietly simple and kind.

Clove: Girl tribute from District 2. Career. Skilled with knives. Tries to kill Katniss, but is killed by Thresh before she can finish the job.

Cornucopia: The site of the opening battle in every Hunger Games. Futuristic horn of plenty, set in a field and overflowing with weapons that tributes may use in the Games — if they can get them without being killed.

Crane, Seneca: Head Gamemaker in the Seventy-fourth Hunger Games.

Dark Days, the: The long-ago rebellion of the districts against the Capitol.

districts: Twelve areas, each dedicated to a different industry, which surround the Capitol and together make up the country of Panem.

Everdeen family plant book: Large scrapbook containing information about properties of herbs and plants. Katniss uses it for reference while foraging in the woods.

Everdeen, Katniss: Sixteen years old, resident of the Seam, District 12. Head of her family. Volunteers as tribute in the Hunger Games when her sister is chosen. A survivor.

Everdeen, Mr.: Katniss's father, killed in a mining explosion when Katniss was eleven. Taught his eldest daughter how to hunt and sing.

Everdeen, Mrs.: Katniss's mother. Fell into a deep depression when her husband died, was unable to care for her daughters. Is better now, but still damaged. Works as a healer.

Everdeen, Primrose: Katniss's beloved twelve-year-old sister. Chosen as tribute in the Hunger Games, until Katniss steps in to take her place.

Flavius: Member of Katniss's prep team. Helps with Katniss's Capitol makeover.

Flickerman, Caesar: Has hosted interviews before and after the Hunger Games for the past forty years. A timeless television personality.

force field: Will repel anything that is thrown at it. One of the Capitol's means of control.

Foxface: Girl tribute from District 5. Sly and elusive. Dies after poaching and eating nightlock berries.

Gamemakers: The team responsible for designing the arena for the Hunger Games, as well as all of the challenges within it. Control the Games from inside their Capitol headquarters.

Glimmer: Girl tribute from District 1. Career. Flirtatious and sexy. Killed by tracker jackers.

groosling: Wild bird that lives inside the arena, and elsewhere in Panem. A food source for tributes in the Games.

Hawthorne, Gale: Eighteen years old. Katniss's best friend and hunting partner. Also from the Seam. Father killed in same mining accident that killed Mr. Everdeen. Promises to care for Katniss's family when she leaves for the Games.

Hob, the: District 12's black market. Katniss sells game here, sometimes even to Peacekeepers.

hovercraft: Capitol airship. Used to transport tributes to the arena and also to take dead tributes away.

Hunger Games, the: Gladiator games developed by the Capitol to keep the districts in line. Two tributes are chosen from each district, one boy and one girl, between the ages of twelve and eighteen. They are sent to an arena to fight to the death on live TV.

jabberjay: Bird muttation with the ability to memorize and repeat human conversation. Developed by the Capitol to use for spying, but not effective. Rebels fed the birds misinformation.

Justice Building, the: The Capitol's headquarters in each district.

katniss: Plant that Katniss was named for. A tuber that grows in water. Tall, with leaves like arrowheads.

Lady: Prim's goat, a birthday gift from Katniss. With Lady's milk, Prim makes and sells cheese.

Marvel: Boy tribute from District 1. Career. Kills Rue. Killed by Katniss.

Mellark, Peeta: Boy tribute from District 12. Once helped Katniss in a crisis, and neither has forgotten. Baker's son. Good with words and people. Has always loved Katniss from afar.

mockingjay: Offspring of male jabberjays and female mockingbirds. Can replicate bird whistles and human melodies. An accidental muttation.

muttations: Genetically altered animals developed by the Capitol to use as weapons. Also known as mutts.

nightlock: Wild berries. Highly poisonous.

Octavia: Member of Katniss's prep team. Helps with Katniss's Capitol makeover.

Panem: Country of the future, where North America used to be, made up of twelve districts and one great Capitol. Setting for *The Hunger Games.*

Peacekeepers: The Capitol's police.

Portia: Peeta's stylist.

reaping: Method of choosing tributes for the Hunger Games. Boys' names are in one giant ball, and girls' names are in another. One name is chosen from each ball, with great fanfare.

Remake Center, the: Where tributes go upon arriving in the Capitol. Here, each tribute is given whatever trimming, shaving, tweezing, or polishing seems necessary, then presented to a stylist.

Rue: Girl tribute from District 11. Small, fast, and agile. Katniss's ally and heartbreak in the arena. Killed by Marvel, setting the stage for Katniss's rebellion.

rue: Small yellow flower that Katniss has seen in District 12.

Seam, the: A shabby neighborhood in District 12, home to many coal miners and their families, including the Everdeens.

silver parachute: Method of sending gifts from Capitol sponsors to tributes in the arena.

Snow, President Coriolanus: President of Panem. Looks kindly and gentle, but is actually brutal and cruel.

Templesmith, Claudius: Longtime announcer for the Hunger Games, along with Caesar Flickerman.

tessera: Purchased by desperate people in the districts. A child can obtain an extra supply of food or oil for his or her family . . . by putting his or her name in the reaping an extra time.

Thresh: Boy tribute from District 11. A gentle giant. Kills Clove because he thinks she killed Rue. Lets Katniss go because of her ties to Rue. Is killed by Cato.

token: Memento taken by tributes into the arena. Usually a reminder of home.

Training Center, the: Where tributes learn the skills they will need to fight — and perhaps survive — in the arena.

tracker jackers: Genetically altered wasps whose sting contains a dangerous venom that causes hallucinations and even death.

Treaty of Treason, the: Ended the rebellion of the districts against the Capitol, setting up the Hunger Games.

Trinket, Effie: Conducts the reaping for District 12 every year, and escorts the district's tributes to the Capitol. Manically upbeat and outlandishly dressed, she always makes a spectacle in District 12.

Venia: Member of Katniss's prep team. Helps with Katniss's Capitol makeover.

Victor's Village: Where victors live when the Hunger Games are over and they return home. Each district has one. In District 12, only one person lives there.

Victory Banquet: After the Games are over, the victor is honored at this celebration.